Rookie
Read-About® Science

Astronauts

By Carmen Bredeson

Consultants
Minna Gretchen Palaquibay
Rose Center for Earth and Space
American Museum of Natural History
New York, New York

Nanci Vargus, Ed.D.
Primary Multiage Teacher
Decatur Township Schools
Indianapolis, Indiana

Katy Kane
Educational Consultant

SCHOLASTIC INC.
New York Toronto London Auckland Sydney
Mexico City New Delhi Hong Kong Buenos Aires

Designer: Herman Adler Design
Photo Researcher: Caroline Anderson
The photo on the cover shows astronaut Michael Lopez-Alegria working
on the International Space Station.

ISBN 0-516-24489-2

12 11 10 9 8 7 6 5 4   6 7 8 9/0

Printed in Mexico.   61

First Scholastic paperback printing, February 2004

Astronauts (AS-truh-nawts)
are men and women who
travel into space.

The first astronauts flew
in small space capsules
(KAP-suhlz). Capsules
are little spaceships.

These little spaceships
held just one person.

Today, astronauts fly
on the space shuttle.

Eight people can fit inside the shuttle.

Astronauts train for more than a year to get ready for a flight. They have special jobs to learn.

The commander (kuh-MAND-ur) is the flight leader. This astronaut flies the shuttle. The commander also makes sure the crew is safe.

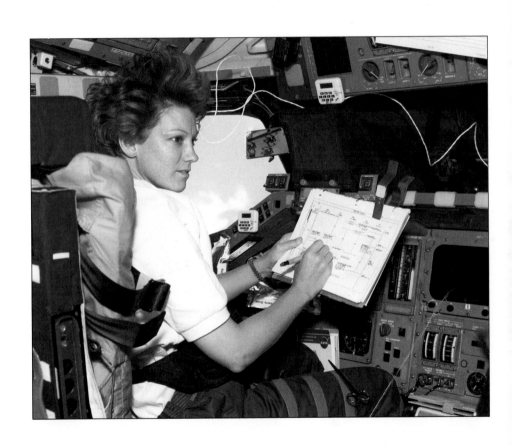

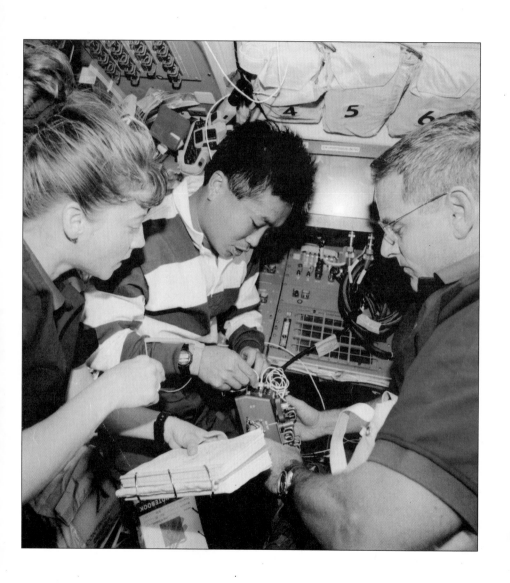

The crew spends months learning how the shuttle works.

What if something breaks in space? The astronauts need to know how to fix it.

Astronauts do science during the flight. Some study how plants grow in space.

15

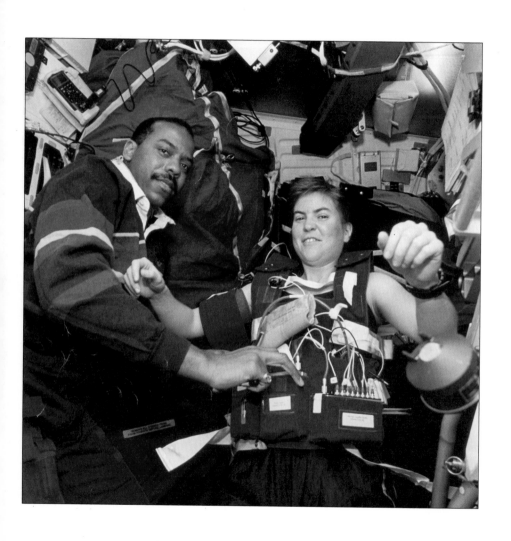

Sometimes, one of the astronauts is a doctor. The doctor does tests on the crew. The doctor wants to learn what being in space does to their bodies.

Astronauts take space
walks outside of the
shuttle. They put on
big space suits to work
in space.

Many astronauts are scientists
or doctors. They must have
college degrees.

They need to be very
healthy, too.

Do you want to be an
astronaut? Study hard
in school.

Exercise and eat good food
to make your body strong.

Today there is something new in space. It is the International (in-tur-NASH-uh-nuhl) Space Station.

The whole station will
take many years to build.

A lot of astronauts will be needed for this work.

Maybe you will be
an astronaut.

Will you work on the
space station?

Will you be the first
person to walk on Mars?

Words You Know

astronaut

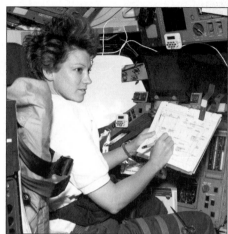

commander

International Space Station

space capsule

space shuttle

space suit

Index

About the Author

Carmen Bredeson has written dozens of nonfiction books for children. She lives in Texas and enjoys traveling and doing research for her books.

Photo Credits

Photographs © 2003: AP/Wide World Photos/NASA: 5; Corbis Images: 11, 30 top right (AFP), 4, 31 top left (Dean Conger), 29 (Richard T. Nowitz), 7, 8 (Roger Ressmeyer), 3, 6, 16, 22, 30 top left, 31 top right; NASA: cover, 12, 15, 19, 20, 21, 25, 26, 27, 30 bottom, 31 bottom; PhotoEdit/David Young-Wolff: 23.